Using Language Well
Book Two

English, Grammar, and Writing Points
from *Spelling Wisdom, Book Two*

Student Book

by Sonya Shafer

Using Language Well, Book Two, Student Book: English, Grammar, and Writing Points from *Spelling Wisdom, Book Two*

Cover Design: John Shafer

ISBN 978-1-61634-314-9 printed
ISBN 978-1-61634-315-6 electronic download

Published by
Simply Charlotte Mason, LLC
930 New Hope Road #11-892
Lawrenceville, Georgia 30045
simplycharlottemason.com

Printed by PrintLogic, Inc.
Monroe, Georgia, USA

Contents

How to Use This Book

Using Language Well, Book Two, is designed to be used alongside *Spelling Wisdom, Book Two*. You will need both books.

Spelling Wisdom books and *Using Language Well* teacher books are non-consumable and can be reused. *Using Language Well* student books are consumable; you will need one per student and a notebook for dictation exercises.

We recommend doing two lessons per week. At that pace this book will last two years: Lessons 1–70 in the first year, Lessons 71–140 in the second.

Most lessons take only five or ten minutes to complete, plus the time spent to prepare for dictation.

Lesson 1

(from Exercise 1, A Book on Hand)

1. Read Exercise 1 in *Spelling Wisdom, Book 2.*

2. One particular word in that sentence is very important. It helps you get the same mental picture that the writer had in her mind when she wrote the sentence. That word is the name of a thing: *book.*

   We call words that name things *nouns*. Think of five different nouns that, if used in that sentence instead of *book*, would change the whole mental picture.

   ____

   ____

   ____

   ____

   ____

Writing Point: *Choose nouns carefully when you are writing to best communicate the picture you have in your head.*

3. Prepare Exercise 1 for dictation by following these steps.

   » Step One: Read the passage and identify which words you don't know how to spell yet.

   » Step Two: Study those words. Look at them carefully until you can close your eyes and see them in your mind.

   » Step Three: Look closely at the punctuation and capital letters. (Copy the exercise, if that will help you.)

   » Step Four: When you are sure you know how to spell every single word in the exercise and are familiar with the punctuation and capitalization, ask your teacher to dictate it to you while you write it in a notebook.

Lesson 2

(from Exercise 2, Great Things)

1. Read Exercise 2 in *Spelling Wisdom, Book 2.*
2. Explain what a noun is.

 ____

 ____

3. Some nouns name things that you can actually see or hear, such as *book* or *music*; other nouns name things that you cannot see or hear, but you know they exist.

 List five nouns from the exercise.

 ____

 ____

 ____

 ____

 ____

4. Prepare Exercise 2 for dictation by following these steps.
 - Step One: Read the passage and identify which words you don't know how to spell yet.
 - Step Two: Study those words. Look at them carefully until you can close your eyes and see them in your mind.
 - Step Three: Look closely at the punctuation and capital letters. (Copy the exercise, if that will help you.)
 - Step Four: When you are sure you know how to spell every single word in the exercise and are familiar with the punctuation and capitalization, ask your teacher to dictate it to you while you write it in your notebook.

Lesson 3

(from Exercise 3, Habits)

1. Read Exercise 3 in *Spelling Wisdom, Book 2.*
2. Define "assumed" in that context.

   ____

   ____

   ____

3. Think of a synonym for each of the words below. (Remember, a synonym is a word that means the same as another word.)

   - strive ______________
   - flayed ______________

4. How would you put the sentence in the exercise in your own words?

   ____

   ____

   ____

5. Prepare Exercise 3 for dictation by following these steps.

   » Step One: Read the passage and identify which words you don't know how to spell yet.

   » Step Two: Study those words. Look at them carefully until you can close your eyes and see them in your mind.

   » Step Three: Look closely at the punctuation and capital letters. (Copy the exercise, if that will help you.)

   » Step Four: When you are sure you know how to spell every single word in the exercise and are familiar with the punctuation and capitalization, ask your teacher to dictate it to you while you write it in your notebook.

Lesson 4

(from Exercise 4, Responsibility)

1. Read Exercise 4 in *Spelling Wisdom, Book 2.*

2. A sentence can be divided into two main parts: the subject (that of which we speak) and the predicate (what we say about it). Divide the sentence from the exercise into its two main parts by drawing a line between the subject and the predicate.

   You cannot escape the responsibility of tomorrow by evading it today.

3. Study the exercise until you are prepared for dictation. Make sure you know how to spell all of the nouns.

Lesson 5

(from Exercise 5, On the Truth)

1. Read Exercise 5 in *Spelling Wisdom, Book 2.*
2. Tell what a noun is.

    ____

    ____

3. Find two nouns in this shortened sentence from the exercise and mark them by writing *N* above each.

    Men occasionally stumble over the truth.

4. Study the exercise until you are prepared for dictation. Make sure you are completing all the steps.
    - Step One: Read the passage and identify which words you don't know how to spell yet.
    - Step Two: Study those words. Look at them carefully until you can close your eyes and see them in your mind.
    - Step Three: Look closely at the punctuation and capital letters. (Copy the exercise, if that will help you.)
    - Step Four: When you are sure you know how to spell every single word in the exercise and are familiar with the punctuation and capitalization, ask your teacher to dictate it to you while you write it in your notebook.

Lesson 6

(from Exercise 6, Ride On)

1. Read Exercise 6 in *Spelling Wisdom, Book 2.*
2. What do the terms *rough-shod* and *smooth-shod* mean? Do a little research and write your findings below.

3. Study the exercise until you are prepared for dictation. Don't forget the hyphens when you spell the two terms you researched.

Lesson 7

(from Exercise 7, You May Deceive)

1. Read Exercise 7 in *Spelling Wisdom, Book 2.*
2. Two nouns are repeated three times each in the exercise. What are they?

   ____

   ____

3. Why did Lincoln repeat those words, do you think? What kind of effect does the repetition have?

   ____

   ____

   ____

4. Study the exercise until you are prepared for dictation.

Lesson 8

(from Exercise 8, On Adversity)

1. Read Exercise 8 in *Spelling Wisdom, Book 2.*
2. Find two nouns in the first line of the exercise.

   ___

   ___

3. The second line contains the little word *it.* To what word in the first line does *it* refer?

   ___

   It is a pronoun. A pronoun is a word that is used in place of a noun. You will find a short list of frequently used pronouns on page 149 in this book.

4. Study the exercise until you are prepared for dictation.

Lesson 9

(from Exercise 9, Exist Today)

1. Read Exercise 9 in *Spelling Wisdom, Book 2.*
2. Tell whether each word below is a noun or pronoun. For each pronoun, tell which noun it takes the place of.

    - roses ______________________
    - they ______________________
    - window ______________________
    - ones ______________________
    - God ______________________
    - reference ______________________

Writing Point: *Pronouns can make a big difference in communicating clearly. Make sure your reader can easily determine which noun any pronoun stands for in your writing.*

3. Study the exercise until you are prepared for dictation. Don't forget to capitalize the word that refers to deity.

Lesson 10

(from Exercise 10, The Rain Ran Wildly)

1. Read Exercise 10 in *Spelling Wisdom, Book 2.*
2. Find an antonym in the exercise for each word below. (Remember, an antonym is a word that means the opposite of another word.)
    - calmly ______________________
    - small ______________________
    - down ______________________
    - slow ______________________
    - without ______________________
3. Study the exercise until you are prepared for dictation.

Lesson 11

(from Exercise 11, On Habits)

1. Read Exercise 11 in *Spelling Wisdom, Book 2.*
2. Tell whether each word below is a noun or pronoun. For each pronoun, tell which noun it takes the place of.

    - mold ______
    - man ______
    - he ______
    - it ______
    - habit ______
    - mirror ______

3. Study the exercise until you are prepared for dictation.

Lesson 12

(from Exercise 12, On Judging)

1. Read Exercise 12 in *Spelling Wisdom, Book 2.*
2. Which pronouns in the exercise refer to the young reader?

____

3. Which pronoun in the exercise refers to the writer?

____

4. Why are there commas around "my son" in the first sentence?

____

____

5. Study the exercise until you are prepared for dictation. Remember to set off the direct address and the word *therefore* with commas.

Writing Point: *That little comma can make a big difference in communicating clearly. It can change the meaning of a sentence from cannibalistic ("It's time to eat my son") to informative ("It's time to eat, my son"). Your readers will thank you for using a comma to make your intention clear!*

Lesson 13

(from Exercise 13, Be Always Ready)

1. Read Exercise 13 in *Spelling Wisdom, Book 2.*
2. Define each word listed below, then without looking at the exercise, determine which homonym from each set belongs in the given statements.

   - to ____________________
   - two ____________________
   - too ____________________

   My religious belief teaches me ____________ feel as safe in battle as in bed.

   - for ____________________
   - four ____________________

   God has fixed the time ____________ my death.

   - do ____________________
   - due ____________________
   - dew ____________________

   I ____________ not concern myself about that, but to be always ready, no matter when it may overtake me.

3. Study the exercise until you are prepared for dictation.

Lesson 14

(from Exercise 14, Life Is Stranger)

1. Read Exercise 14 in *Spelling Wisdom, Book 2.*
2. Tell what a noun is.

   ____

   ____

3. There are two kinds of nouns, and the exercise contains them both: common and proper. Common nouns refer to any one of a class of persons, places, or things. Proper nouns name particular persons, places, or things.

   In the list of nouns below, taken from the exercise, identify which are common and which are proper.

   - fellow ____________________
   - fire ____________________
   - Sherlock Holmes ____________________
   - life ____________________
   - lodgings ____________________
   - Baker Street ____________________
   - mind ____________________

4. What do you notice about the beginning letters of the proper nouns?

   ____

   ____

5. Study the exercise until you are prepared for dictation. Look closely at the punctuation that sets off what Sherlock Holmes said. (Note: There is no closing quotation mark because Holmes continues to talk; the exercise stops before you can see the rest of what he said. Read the book to find out the rest.)

Lesson 15

(from Exercise 15, The Ditch)

1. Read Exercise 15 in *Spelling Wisdom, Book 2.*
2. In the list of nouns below, identify which are common and which are proper.

    - book ______________________________
    - The Pilgrim's Progress ______________________________
    - author ______________________________
    - John Bunyan ______________________________

3. Give proper nouns suggested to you by each of the following common nouns. Be sure to capitalize your proper nouns.

    - city ______________________________
    - country ______________________________
    - street ______________________________
    - author ______________________________
    - artist ______________________________

4. Study the exercise until you are prepared for dictation.

Lesson 16

(from Exercise 16, A Man Said to the Universe)

1. Read Exercise 16 in *Spelling Wisdom, Book 2.*

2. Give the common noun that each of the following pronouns stands for in the exercise:

    - I ____________________

    - me ____________________

3. Look at the first two lines of the exercise. Identify each mark of punctuation in that sentence from the exercise and explain why it is used.

    - universe, ____________________

    - "Sir ____________________

    - Sir, ____________________

    - exist!" ____________________

    ____

Writing Point: *Punctuation is a tool that you can use in your writing to help your reader understand precisely what you are trying to communicate. Correct punctuation eliminates confusion.*

4. Study the exercise until you are prepared for dictation. Look closely at the punctuation around the quoted material and the dialogue tags.

Lesson 17

(from Exercise 17, Michelangelo)

1. Read Exercise 17 in *Spelling Wisdom, Book 2.*
2. In the exercise, find the following:
    - a common noun ______________________________
    - a proper noun ______________________________
    - the common noun that is related to the proper noun ______________________________
    - the pronoun that stands for the critic ______________________________
    - the pronoun that stands for the strange man ______________________________
    - another common noun ______________________________
3. Study the exercise until you are prepared for dictation. Note the dash that sets off the expanded explanation.

Lesson 18

(from Exercise 18, Cautious Utterance)

1. Read Exercise 18 in *Spelling Wisdom, Book 2.*
2. Just as nouns can be singular or plural, referring to one or more than one thing, so pronouns can be singular or plural. For the nouns and pronouns from the exercise listed below, tell whether each is singular or plural.

   - things ______________________
   - world ______________________
   - we ______________________
   - our ______________________
   - feet ______________________

Writing Point: *One way you can help your reader mentally connect the pronouns to their corresponding nouns in your writing is to make sure each pair matches in number; a singular pronoun logically connects to a singular noun, and a plural pronoun represents a plural noun.*

3. Study the exercise until you are prepared for dictation. Be sure to capitalize the proper noun.

Lesson 19

(from Exercise 19, Equal 100)

1. Read Exercise 19 in *Spelling Wisdom, Book 2.*

2. Tell whether each word below is a noun or pronoun and whether it is singular or plural. For each pronoun, tell which noun in the exercise it takes the place of. (That noun is called the *antecedent.*)

    - signs ________________________________
    - they ________________________________
    - solution ________________________________
    - arrangement ________________________________

3. Can you solve the math challenge?

    ____

    ____

4. Study the exercise until you are prepared for dictation. Notice when a number is spelled with letters and when it is written with numerals.

Lesson 20

(from Exercise 20, Sparrows)

1. Read Exercise 20 in *Spelling Wisdom, Book 2.*
2. Find five nouns in the exercise.

   ____

   ____

   ____

   ____

   ____

3. Divide this shortened sentence from the exercise into its two main parts by drawing a line between the subject and the predicate.

   Sparrows are such gregarious birds.

4. Study the exercise until you are prepared for dictation. Make sure you are completing all the steps.

   » Step One: Read the passage and identify which words you don't know how to spell yet.

   » Step Two: Study those words. Look at them carefully until you can close your eyes and see them in your mind.

   » Step Three: Look closely at the punctuation and capital letters. (Copy the exercise, if that will help you.)

   » Step Four: When you are sure you know how to spell every single word in the exercise and are familiar with the punctuation and capitalization, ask your teacher to dictate it to you while you write it in your notebook.

Lesson 21

(from Exercise 21, The Punctual Servant)

1. Read Exercise 21 in *Spelling Wisdom, Book 2.*
2. Find two proper nouns in the exercise.

   ____

   ____

3. Near the end of the exercise, Mr. Pickwick performed three actions. List them here.

   ____

   ____

   ____

   If you turn the spotlight on just the first word in each description, you will see three verbs: *burst, threw, opened.* A *verb* is a word that tells what the subject is or what the subject does.

   Verbs are so important that you cannot make sense without them. If you omit the verb, you do not know what Mr. Pickwick did: "Mr. Samuel Pickwick ___ like another sun . . . ." You do not know whether he *shone* or *rose* or *set*, or what he did. *Verb* means *word*, for it is the most important word in the sentence. In fact, to make a sentence you must have a verb.

4. Study the exercise until you are prepared for dictation. Pay close attention to the numbers' spellings and hyphenation.

Lesson 22

(from Exercise 22, The Printing Press)

1. Read Exercise 22 in *Spelling Wisdom, Book 2.*
2. In the following sentences from the exercise, identify what part of speech each italicized word is. Write PRO above a pronoun, N above a common noun, PN above a proper noun, and V above a verb.

   Through *it*, *God* will *spread His* Word.

   A spring of *truth* shall *flow* from it.

3. Study the exercise until you are prepared for dictation. The three dots in the second line are called an *ellipsis* and indicate omitted words. Be sure to note where they belong; also notice that the exercise is a quotation by Gutenberg.

Lesson 23

(from Exercise 23, Introspective Music)

1. Read Exercise 23 in *Spelling Wisdom, Book 2.*

2. The verbs that you have studied thus far are verbs that assert action. Identify what part of speech each italicized word is in the following shortened sentences from the exercise. Write PRO above a pronoun, N above a common noun, PN above a proper noun, and AV above an action verb.

   Then *put* on *your* hat and *come*.

   I *observe* that there is a good deal of German *music* on the *program*.

   ***I want* to introspect.**

   Writing Point: *Just as the nouns you choose can change the mental picture in your reader's mind, so can the verbs. Select precise verbs to best communicate clearly.*

3. Study the exercise until you are prepared for dictation. Notice that the entire exercise is a quotation.

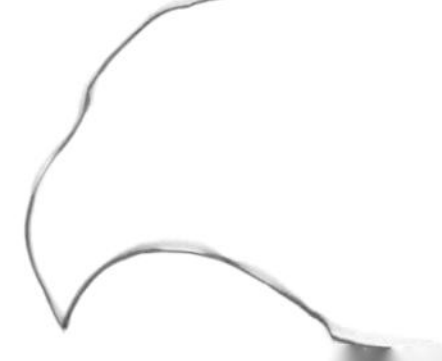

Lesson 24

(from Exercise 24, A Riddle)

1. Read Exercise 24 in *Spelling Wisdom, Book 2.*
2. Find the pronouns and action verbs in the following shortened sentences from the exercise. Write PRO above a pronoun and AV above an action verb.

   Though blind, I enlighten.

   I sing without voice.

   Some love me too fondly.

   I sometimes live ages.

3. Have you figured out the answer to the riddle?

   ____

4. Study the exercise until you are prepared for dictation. Notice especially where the contractions *I'm* and *I've* are used and the two dashes.

Lesson 25

(from Exercise 25, Beginning of a Day)

1. Read Exercise 25 in *Spelling Wisdom, Book 2.*

2. There are some verbs that do not assert action; as, "Mary *was* absent" or "I *am* cheerful." In those sentences *Mary* and *I* are not doing anything; instead, they are being something, and the verbs link the subjects to the descriptions of what they are being. We call that type of verb a *linking verb.* Identify the nouns and linking verbs in the following shortened sentences from the exercise. If the italicized word is a noun, write either N for common noun or PN for proper noun above it; if the italicized word is a linking verb, write LV.

   It *was* the beginning of a *day* in *June.*

   The *streets were* nearly free from passengers.

   The *houses* and *shops were* closed.

3. Study the exercise until you are prepared for dictation. Make sure you spell *teeming* correctly.

Lesson 26

(from Exercise 26, Want to Work)

1. Read Exercise 26 in *Spelling Wisdom, Book 2.*
2. Give the antecedent (see Lesson 19) for each of the following pronouns from the exercise and tell whether each is singular or plural:
   - my ____________________
   - she ____________________
   - who ____________________
   - them ____________________
3. Notice what punctuation is used after the salutation in a business letter.

   ____
4. How does that differ from the punctuation in a personal letter?

   ____

   ____
5. Study the exercise until you are prepared for dictation. Be ready to write it in letter format.

Lesson 27

(from Exercise 27, Village in Japan)

1. Read Exercise 27 in *Spelling Wisdom, Book 2.*
2. Identify what part of speech each italicized word is in the following shortened sentences from the exercise. Write PRO above a pronoun, N above a common noun, PN above a proper noun, AV above an action verb, and LV above a linking verb.

There is a certain *village* in *Japan*.

The *sun is* nearer to the inhabitants every noon.

3. Can you solve the math puzzle?

____

____

____

____

4. Study the exercise until you are prepared for dictation.

Lesson 28

(from Exercise 28, The Lounging Figure)

1. Read Exercise 28 in *Spelling Wisdom, Book 2.*
2. Identify what part of speech each italicized word is in the following sentence from the exercise. Write PRO above a pronoun, N above a common noun, PN above a proper noun, AV above an action verb, and LV above a linking verb.

Holmes slowly _reopened his eyes_ and _looked_ impatiently at _his_ gigantic _client._

3. Study the exercise until you are prepared for dictation. Make sure you are completing all the steps.
   - » Step One: Read the passage and identify which words you don't know how to spell yet.
   - » Step Two: Study those words. Look at them carefully until you can close your eyes and see them in your mind.
   - » Step Three: Look closely at the punctuation and capital letters. (Copy the exercise, if that will help you.)
   - » Step Four: When you are sure you know how to spell every single word in the exercise and are familiar with the punctuation and capitalization, ask your teacher to dictate it to you while you write it in your notebook.

Lesson 29

(from Exercise 29, Heaven Above Was Blue)

1. Read Exercise 29 in *Spelling Wisdom, Book 2.*
2. For each shortened sentence below, tell whether the italicized verb is an action verb (AV) or a linking verb (LV).

Heaven above *was* blue.

Earth beneath *was* green.

The river *glistened* like a path of diamonds in the sun.

The birds *poured* forth their songs from the shady trees.

The lark *soared* high above the waving corn.

The deep buzz of insects *filled* the air.

Writing Point: *Linking verbs are important; but if you use only linking verbs, your writing can convey a very passive tone with little action or imagination. Action verbs add flavor to your writing.*

3. Study the exercise until you are prepared for dictation. Be sure to put the semicolons in place of periods to separate the complete thoughts.

Lesson 30

(from Exercise 30, The Beatitudes)

1. Read Exercise 30 in *Spelling Wisdom, Book 2.*
2. Look closely at the final paragraph of those words of Jesus. To whom is each of these pronouns referring?

    - you ______________________________
    - my ______________________________
    - your ______________________________
    - they ______________________________
    - which ______________________________

3. Notice the apostrophe with the word *righteousness*. Why is it there?

    ____

    ____

4. Why is there no *s* after the apostrophe?

    ____

    ____

5. Study the exercise until you are prepared for dictation. Be sure to include the apostrophe in *righteousness' sake.*

Lesson 31

(from Exercise 31, Hearty Laugh)

1. Read Exercise 31 in *Spelling Wisdom, Book 2.*
2. Identify what part of speech each italicized word is in the following sentences from the exercise. Write PRO above a pronoun, N above a common noun, PN above a proper noun, AV above an action verb, and LV above a linking verb. (Hint: Be careful with the first verb. Determine whether it denotes an action Holmes did or links him to a description that follows later in the sentence.)

   Sherlock Holmes looked **deeply chagrined.**

   A few yards off *he stopped* under a lamppost and *laughed* in the hearty, noiseless fashion

   which was **peculiar to *him*.**

3. Study the exercise until you are prepared for dictation.

Lesson 32

(from Exercise 32, The True Workman)

1. Read Exercise 32 in *Spelling Wisdom, Book 2.*
2. Define each word listed below, then determine which homonym from each set belongs in the given statements from recent exercises.

   - wait____
   - weight ____
   - pain____
   - pane____

   But were we burdened with like ______________ of ______________,

   As much or more we should ourselves complain.

   In all these matters the true workman will ______________ for the Master's beck, glance, or signal before a step is taken.

   - threw ____
   - through ____

   He drew a sovereign from his pocket and ______________ it down upon the slab, turning away with the air of a man whose disgust is too deep for words.

   - led ____
   - lead ____

   That ditch is it into which the blind have ______________ the blind in all ages and have both there miserably perished.

3. Study the exercise until you are prepared for dictation.

Lesson 33

(from Exercise 33, This Is Your Victory)

1. Read Exercise 33 in *Spelling Wisdom, Book 2.*
2. Find the pronoun in the middle of the speech that refers to all the men and women.

   ____

3. Is that pronoun singular or plural?

   ____

   If the antecedent is singular, the pronoun that replaces it should also be singular. If the antecedent is plural, its pronoun should be plural too. It is important that their numbers agree.

4. Find two proper nouns in the exercise.

   ____

5. Study the exercise until you are prepared for dictation. When World War II ended in Europe, Winston Churchill gave this brief speech from a balcony to a large crowd that had gathered in England's streets. After he spoke those opening words, "This is your victory," the celebrating people interrupted and cried, "No, it is yours!" Churchill had courageously led them through many dark days.

Lesson 34

(from Exercise 34, The City)

1. Read Exercise 34 in *Spelling Wisdom, Book 2.*
2. Why are there two semicolons in the first sentence? What job are they performing?

    ____

    ____

3. What kind of verbs are used in that first sentence: action or linking?

    ____

4. Find five common nouns in the exercise.

    ____

    ____

    ____

    ____

    ____

5. Study the exercise until you are prepared for dictation.

Lesson 35

(from Exercise 35, Signature with a Sentiment)

1. Read Exercise 35 in *Spelling Wisdom, Book 2.*
2. Explain why each mark of punctuation is used in the exercise.

    - Jan. ____________________
    - 5, ____________________
    - Dear Sir: ____________________
    - "signature with a sentiment" ____________________
    - mislaid. ____________________
    - man; ____________________
    - than I, ____________________
    - names. ____________________
    - Very respectfully, ____________________

3. Study the exercise until you are prepared for dictation. Be sure to write it in letter format.

Lesson 36

(from Exercise 36, An Ivory Miniature)

1. Read Exercise 36 in *Spelling Wisdom, Book 2.*

2. The same verb is used twice in the exercise. Can you find it?

   ____

   Did you notice that the second time it is used, it is part of a verb phrase? Another small verb has been added to the main verb in order to help it convey a more accurate sense of time: *had.* When a verb is popped into place to help the main verb, it is called a *helping verb.* With it in place, we know that the artist had finished his work previously. You will find a short list of frequently used helping verbs on page 149.

3. Study the exercise until you are prepared for dictation. Notice that the first sentence is quoted material with no dialogue tag.

Lesson 37

(from Exercise 37, Paris)

1. Read Exercise 37 in *Spelling Wisdom, Book 2.*

2. The semicolons in that exercise are doing an entirely different job from the semicolons in Exercise 34. In Exercise 34 they are separating complete sentences instead of using periods. Here they are separating items in a series. Why couldn't commas be used to do that job in the sentence in Exercise 37? (Hint: Look carefully at the third item in the series.)

____

____

____

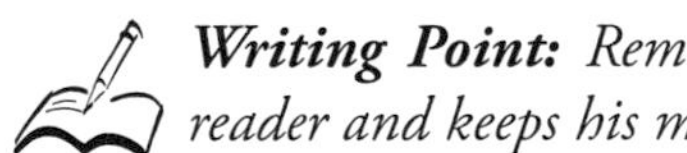

Writing Point: *Remember, correct punctuation eliminates confusion for your reader and keeps his mind on your ideas communicated through words.*

3. Study the exercise until you are prepared for dictation. Be careful to get the commas and semicolons in the correct places.

Lesson 38

(from Exercise 38, Seal Lullaby)

1. Read Exercise 38 in *Spelling Wisdom, Book 2.*
2. Notice the different time frames implied by the verbs that are used in the poem. For each phrase, identify whether the italicized verb denotes the present, the past, or the future.

   - "black *are* the waters" denotes the present
   - "waters that *sparkled* so green" denotes the ______________________
   - "the moon *looks* downward" denotes the ______________________
   - "billow *meets* billow" denotes the ______________________
   - "the storm *shall* not *wake* thee" denotes the ______________________

3. Study the exercise until you are prepared for dictation. Take some time to read it aloud and enjoy Kipling's use of words!

Lesson 39

(from Exercise 39, Durer)

1. Read Exercise 39 in *Spelling Wisdom, Book 2.*
2. You have learned about the three kinds of verbs. Tell what each one does.
    - Action verbs ____________________
    - Linking verbs ____________________

      ____
    - Helping verbs ____________________

      ____
3. Identify which kind of verb is italicized in the shortened sentences from the exercise below. Write AV above each action verb, LV above each linking verb, and HV above each helping verb.

    Till Durer's time, however, there *had been* little painting that could be regarded as art.

    He *was* above all things patriotic and dearly *loved* his home.
4. Study the exercise until you are prepared for dictation.

Lesson 40

(from Exercise 40, Scenery)

1. Read Exercise 40 in *Spelling Wisdom, Book 2.*
2. Identify which kind of verb is italicized in the shortened sentences from the exercise below. Write AV above each action verb, LV above each linking verb, and HV above each helping verb.

He *lowered* the window and *looked* out at the rising sun. There *was* a ridge of ploughed land

with a plough upon it where it *had been left* last night when the horses *were unyoked.*

3. Study the exercise until you are prepared for dictation. (You might see the word *plough* also spelled *plow* sometimes.)

Lesson 41

(from Exercise 41, His Main Fault)

1. Read Exercise 41 in *Spelling Wisdom, Book 2.*
2. Identify which kind of verb is italicized in the shortened sentences from the exercise below. Write AV above each action verb, LV above each linking verb, and HV above each helping verb.

"Oh, he has his faults too," *said* Mr. Wilson.

He *ought to be improving* his mind.

That *is* his main fault.

3. Why is there an apostrophe in *he's* and in *There's*?

____

____

4. Study the exercise until you are prepared for dictation. Pay special attention to the punctuation around the quoted material and the dialogue tag.

Lesson 42

(from Exercise 42, Times That Try Men's Souls)

1. Read Exercise 42 in *Spelling Wisdom, Book 2.*
2. Identify what part of speech each italicized word is in the following sentences from the exercise. Write PRO above a pronoun, N above a common noun, PN above a proper noun, AV above an action verb, LV above a linking verb, and HV above a helping verb.

These are the times that try men's souls. The summer _soldier_ and the sunshine patriot _will_, in this crisis, _shrink_ from the _service_ of _their_ country; but _he_ that _stands_ it now _deserves_ the _love_ and thanks of man and woman.

3. Why is there an apostrophe in *men's*?

____

4. Study the exercise until you are prepared for dictation. Do you agree with Thomas Paine's ideas presented in the exercise? He wrote those words during the days of the American Revolution.

Lesson 43

(from Exercise 43, Stained Glass)

1. Read Exercise 43 in *Spelling Wisdom, Book 2.*
2. Explain why the following commas are in the exercise. What jobs are they doing?
   - Lincoln, ________________
   - England, ________________
   - little bits of time, of knowledge, and of opportunities ________________
3. In each phrase from the exercise below, identify which kind of verb is italicized (action, linking, helping) and which time frame is implied (past, present, future).
   - There *is* a window of stained glass ________________
   - which *was made* by an apprentice ________________
   - We *may do* work for God ________________

   When we talk about which time frame is implied, we call that the *tense* of the verb. We say that a verb is in present tense, past tense, or future tense.
4. Study the exercise until you are prepared for dictation. Be sure to capitalize the proper nouns.

Lesson 44

(from Exercise 44, To Speak in Public)

1. Read Exercise 44 in *Spelling Wisdom, Book 2.*
2. Sometimes verbs try to hide. Look at the contraction in the exercise and tell of what two words that contraction is made.

   ____________ ____

3. To make it even more interesting, the second word of that contraction is actually a helping verb. Look for the main verb it is helping in that quotation.

   ____

4. Summarize two important techniques you learned for finding verbs in sentences:
   - Think of each contraction as ________________________________
   - Sometimes verb phrases can be interrupted by ________________________________

Writing Point: *Make sure your verb phrases communicate exactly what you mean them to, especially when pairing one with a contraction. Your writing represents you.*

5. Study the exercise until you are prepared for dictation. Notice the dash in the middle of the exercise that is setting off additional explanation.

Lesson 45

(from Exercise 45, A Strange Procession)

1. Read Exercise 45 in *Spelling Wisdom, Book 2.*
2. In the first sentence, what word is used to describe the blaze? ____________

    • its gleams? ____________

    • the light of the torches? ____________

3. In the rest of the exercise, which noun is described as strange? ____________

    • dozen? ____________

    • principal? ____________

    Words that describe nouns—that affect the meaning, or modify them—are called *adjectives.*

4. Study the exercise until you are prepared for dictation. Be sure you spell *Councilor* and *principal* correctly; they both have homonyms that can easily be confused.

Lesson 46

(from Exercise 46, Forbearance)

1. Read Exercise 46 in *Spelling Wisdom, Book 2.*
2. What adjective in the exercise describes the noun *behavior*?

3. What does *pulse* mean in that context? Define that word.

4. Find the possessive word in the second line.

5. What is the difference between *its* and *it's*?

Writing Point: *Words are to a writer what paint is to an artist; they are your tools to help you communicate exactly what you have in your mind. The more words you know—with their possible definitions—the more tools you will have ready at hand to use.*

6. Study the exercise until you are prepared for dictation.

Lesson 47

(from Exercise 47, The Heart That Feels Not)

1. Read Exercise 47 in *Spelling Wisdom, Book 2.*

2. Identify what part of speech each italicized word is in the following sentence from the exercise. Write PRO above a pronoun, N above a common noun, PN above a proper noun, AV above an action verb, LV above a linking verb, HV above a helping verb, ADJ above an adjective. (Hint: Sometimes adjectives come after the noun or pronoun they are describing.)

   ***It* is the business of *little* minds to shrink; but he whose *heart is firm* and *whose* conscience**

   ***approves his conduct will pursue* his principles unto death.**

3. Study the exercise until you are prepared for dictation. More strong words from Thomas Paine!

Lesson 48

(from Exercise 48, A Gram)

1. Read Exercise 48 in *Spelling Wisdom, Book 2.*
2. Identify which kind of verb is italicized in the sentences from the exercise below. Write AV above an action verb, LV above a linking verb, and HV above a helping verb.

A gram *is* a way to measure volume, or mass.

Vitamins *are* often *measured* in milligrams. *Look* at the label of any vitamin bottle in your house and *see* how many milligrams you *can find.*

3. Find the adjective that describes *bottle* in the last sentence given above.

____

4. List the two contractions in the exercise and tell of what words each is comprised.

____

____

5. Study the exercise until you are prepared for dictation. Notice that there is only one period after the abbreviation even though it is at the end of the sentence.

Lesson 49

(from Exercise 49, A Favorite Game)

1. Read Exercise 49 in *Spelling Wisdom, Book 2.*
2. For each verb from the exercise below, tell what kind it is.

    - were playing ______________________________
    - added ______________________________
    - liked ______________________________
    - were ______________________________

3. Find three proper nouns in the exercise.

    ____

    ____

    ____

4. Find the adjectives that modify the nouns listed below.

    ______________________________ sisters

    ______________________________ tiles

    ______________________________ sports

5. Study the exercise until you are prepared for dictation. Be watchful for the quotation marks around particular words.

Lesson 50

(from Exercise 50, Upbraiding)

1. Read Exercise 50 in *Spelling Wisdom, Book 2.*
2. The exercise is part of a script. What do you notice about the format that tells us that fact?

   ____

   ____

3. What scenario do you think is being played out in the scene from which the excerpt is taken?

   ____

   ____

   ____

4. Find three adjectives in Cousin's second sentence. List each adjective below with its following noun.

   ____

   ____

   ____

5. Study the exercise until you are prepared for dictation. Be sure to write it in script format.

Lesson 51

(from Exercise 51, Tom As Robin Hood)

1. Read Exercise 51 in *Spelling Wisdom, Book 2.*
2. An easy way to find an adjective is to ask, "Which (noun or pronoun)?" Give it a try with these nouns in the exercise.

   - Which *nun*? ______________________________
   - Which *wound*? ______________________________
   - Which *outlaws*? ______________________________
   - Which *hands*? ______________________________
   - Which *tree*? ______________________________

Writing Point: *How would that passage communicate a different mental picture if the adjectives were different? Try changing some of them and see for yourself the effect it has.*

3. Tom and his companions are attempting to act out the death of Robin Hood, as told in *The Merry Adventures of Robin Hood*—a wonderful book! Study the exercise until you are prepared for dictation. Watch for the quoted material and dialogue tag near the end.

Lesson 52

(from Exercise 52, The Signs of the Seasons)

1. Read Exercise 52 in *Spelling Wisdom, Book 2.*
2. For each word from the exercise listed below give two definitions, each according to which part of speech is specified. Then determine which definition fits best in the line from the poem and label it with its correct part of speech. Here's an example:

   - stand (verb) to balance upright on one's legs
   - stand (noun) a structure used to display one or more items

   V

   When cattle *stand* under the shady trees

   - nest (verb) ______________________________
   - nest (noun) ______________________________

   when the bluebird comes And builds its *nest*

   - steer (noun) ______________________________
   - steer (verb) ______________________________

   And away to the south the robins *steer*

   - mean (verb) ______________________________
   - mean (adjective) ______________________________

   What does it *mean* when days are short

3. Study the exercise until you are prepared for dictation. Look for a pattern to help you remember where the dashes are located in the poem.

Lesson 53

(from Exercise 53, Picking Strawberries)

1. Read Exercise 53 in *Spelling Wisdom, Book 2.*

2. Find the words that identify these nouns in the exercise. The word will come immediately before each noun.

    ______________________ garage

    ______________________ house

    ______________________ table

    ______________________ chair

    ______________________ fan

    ______________________ berry

    ______________________ bowl

    ______________________ spoon

    The words *a*, *an*, and *the* are called *articles*. You will see them often.

3. Is Exercise 53 written in present tense, past tense, or future tense? (Hint: Look at the verbs.)

    ____

4. Study the exercise until you are prepared for dictation.

Lesson 54

(from Exercise 54, The Actress)

1. Read Exercise 54 in *Spelling Wisdom, Book 2.*

2. Identify what part of speech each italicized word is in the following sentence from the exercise. Write PRO above a pronoun, N above a common noun, PN above a proper noun, AV above an action verb, LV above a linking verb, HV above a helping verb, ADJ above an adjective, and ART above an article.

   The actress sat **in** ***the waiting room***; ***her head had begun*** **to ache.**

3. Demonstrate how to properly punctuate a sentence when the dialogue tag comes after the quoted material.

   Quoted material dialogue tag

4. Why is there an apostrophe in *couldn't*?

   ____

   in *producer's*? ____

5. Study the exercise until you are prepared for dictation.

Lesson 55

(from Exercise 55, Two Trains)

1. Read Exercise 55 in *Spelling Wisdom, Book 2.*
2. Find the adjective or article that modifies each of these nouns or pronouns in the exercise.

    ______________________ question

    ______________________ stationmaster

    ______________________ answer

    ______________________other

3. List three proper nouns from the exercise.

    ____

4. See if you can solve the mathematical puzzle.

    ____

    ____

5. Study the exercise until you are prepared for dictation.

Lesson 56

(from Exercise 56, Tobogganing)

1. Read Exercise 56 in *Spelling Wisdom, Book 2.*
2. Look at the second sentence in the exercise and find a possessive word. Is that word singular possessive or plural possessive? How can you tell?

   ____

   ____

3. Identify what part of speech each italicized word is in the following sentence from the exercise. Write PRO above a pronoun, N above a common noun, PN above a proper noun, AV above an action verb, LV above a linking verb, HV above a helping verb, ADJ above an adjective, and ART above an article.

   Our favorite amusement **during** ***that winter was*** **tobogganing.**

4. Did you notice any pronouns that are acting as adjectives?

   ____

   Sometimes they do that. You may mark them with either PRO or ADJ; your choice.

5. Study the exercise until you are prepared for dictation. Note which sentences are exclamatory. (Keep in mind that Helen Keller was both deaf and blind. Can you imagine tobogganing as a blind and deaf person?)

Lesson 57

(from Exercise 57, A Wolf in Sheep's Clothing)

1. Read Exercise 57 in *Spelling Wisdom, Book 2.*
2. Pay close attention to the variety of possessive words found in the exercise. Find the possessive pronoun in the first sentence. Write it here and tell whether it is singular or plural.

   ____

   What noun does it refer to and what does it possess?

   ____

3. Find the possessive pronoun in the second sentence. Write it here and tell whether it is singular or plural.

   ____

   What is its antecedent (the noun to which it refers) and what does it possess?

   ____

4. Explain the difference between *its* and *it's*.

   ____

   ____

5. Find two possessive words in the final sentence: one is a pronoun and one is a common noun.

   ____

   Is the pronoun singular or plural? How can you tell?

   ____

6. Explain the difference between *whose* and *who's*.

   ____

   ____

7. Study the exercise until you are prepared for dictation.

Lesson 58

(from Exercise 58, God Directs All Things)

1. Read Exercise 58 in *Spelling Wisdom, Book 2.*
2. Identify what part of speech each italicized word is in the following sentence from the exercise. Write PRO above a pronoun, N above a common noun, PN above a proper noun, AV above an action verb, LV above a linking verb, HV above a helping verb, ADJ above an adjective, and ART above an article.

The *history* of my life *will say* to *the* world what *it says* to *me*: There *is a loving God, who directs* all things for the best.

3. Why is there a colon in the final sentence? What job does it do?

____

____

4. Study the exercise until you are prepared for dictation.

Lesson 59

(from Exercise 59, The Pilgrims)

1. Read Exercise 59 in *Spelling Wisdom, Book 2.*

2. Find the ten proper nouns in the exercise and list them in alphabetical order. When you alphabetize a person's name, list and arrange that entry as *Last, First,* such as *Smith, Captain John.*

3. In the first sentence, notice what punctuation should be used when writing a compound number (a number comprised of two words).

4. Study the exercise until you are prepared for dictation.

Lesson 60

(from Exercise 60, March)

1. Read Exercise 60 in *Spelling Wisdom, Book 2.*
2. Define each word listed below, then without looking at the exercise, determine which homonym from each set belongs in the given lines from the poem.

   - there ______________________________
   - their ______________________________
   - they're ______________________________

   ______________ **heads never raising;**

   ______________ **is joy in the mountains;**

   - fare ______________________________
   - fair ______________________________

   And now doth ______________ **ill**

   - bear ______________________________
   - bare ______________________________

   On the top of the ______________ **hill;**

Writing Point: *A great way to check whether you should use* their *or* they're *in a sentence is to think about the two words that* they're *stands for:* they are. *If those two words make sense inserted at that place in the sentence, use the contraction.*

3. What does *anon* mean?

   ____

4. Study the exercise until you are prepared for dictation.

Lesson 61

(from Exercise 61, Same Product)

1. Read Exercise 61 in *Spelling Wisdom, Book 2.*
2. Find an action verb that stands alone in the exercise with no helping verbs.

   ____

3. Find a linking verb.

   ____

4. Find a helping verb and write the entire verb phrase.

   ____

5. Find a pronoun and write it along with its antecedent.

   ____

6. Find an article, along with the word it modifies.

   ____

7. Find an adjective modifying a noun.

   ____

8. Can you determine the solutions to the math challenge?

   ____

   ____

9. Study the exercise until you are prepared for dictation.

Lesson 62

(from Exercise 62, The Short-Billed Wren)

1. Read Exercise 62 in *Spelling Wisdom, Book 2.*
2. Find the adjective that modifies each of these nouns in the first sentence of the exercise.

   ______________________________ blackbirds

   ______________________________ pastures

   ______________________________ woods

   ______________________________ wren

   ______________________________ cousin

3. Adjectives made up of more than one word—as, *red-winged*—are called compound adjectives. Notice the punctuation that should be used when writing a compound adjective in order to avoid confusion.

   ____

> ***Writing Point:*** *Without the hyphen in* red-winged blackbird, *the reader would think the writer was referring to a blackbird that was red and had wings—a red winged blackbird. The reader could be distracted pondering such mental puzzles as* How can a blackbird be red? *and* Don't all blackbirds have wings? *Keep your reader focused, not distracted, by using correct punctuation to help him.*

4. Study the exercise until you are prepared for dictation.

Lesson 63

(from Exercise 63, Repairing the Woodman)

1. Read Exercise 63 in *Spelling Wisdom, Book 2.*
2. Find the antecedent for each of these pronouns in the exercise and tell whether each is singular or plural.

    - they ____
    - he ____
    - his ____
    - him ____

    Which antecedent is a proper noun and which is a common noun? Label the corresponding words you wrote with PN or N.

3. Study the exercise until you are prepared for dictation. The word *soldering* is pronounced SOD-er-ing; don't confuse it with military *soldiering*.

Lesson 64

(from Exercise 64, Myles Standish)

1. Read Exercise 64 in *Spelling Wisdom, Book 2.*
2. Find the adjective that modifies each of these nouns in the exercise, then think of a synonym and an antonym for each adjective. Be sure to take into account the context in which the word is used.

Adjective	Synonym	Antonym
______ *family*	______	______
______ *band*	______	______
______ *temper*	______	______

Writing Point: *Thinking of synonyms and antonyms is a great way to come up with the best word selection to convey your precise meaning.*

3. Is Exercise 64 written in present tense, past tense, or future tense?

______

4. Study the exercise until you are prepared for dictation.

Lesson 65

(from Exercise 65, Three-Letter Words)

1. Read Exercise 65 in *Spelling Wisdom, Book 2.*
2. What job are the quotation marks doing in the exercise?

____

____

3. What job is the colon doing?

____

____

4. Why is there a hyphen joining *three* and *letter*?

____

____

5. Study the exercise until you are prepared for dictation. Notice especially that commas and periods always go inside the quotation marks.

Lesson 66

(from Exercise 66, The Wayfarer)

1. Read Exercise 66 in *Spelling Wisdom, Book 2.*
2. Identify what part of speech each italicized word is in the following lines from the poem. Write PRO above a pronoun, N above a common noun, PN above a proper noun, AV above an action verb, LV above a linking verb, HV above a helping verb, ADJ above an adjective, and ART above an article.

Later *he saw* that each *weed*

***Was a singular* knife.**

3. Study the exercise until you are prepared for dictation. You have a double challenge with the dialogue punctuation and the capitalization of each new line in the poem—sometimes in the middle of a sentence. Pay close attention.

Lesson 67

(from Exercise 67, Dorothy's House)

1. Read Exercise 67 in *Spelling Wisdom, Book 2.*
2. Find the possessive pronoun in the second sentence. Write it here and tell whether it's singular or plural.

   ____

3. What is its antecedent?

   ____

4. Find the word in the next sentence that is its homonym.

   ____

5. Define both of those homonyms.

   ____

   ____

6. Find the verb that goes with *ladder*.

   ____

7. Make sure you spell all of those words correctly as you study the exercise and prepare for dictation.

Lesson 68

(from Exercise 68, The Maryland Yellowthroat)

1. Read Exercise 68 in *Spelling Wisdom, Book 2.*
2. Is Exercise 68 written in present tense, past tense, or future tense?

   ____

3. Look at the title of the exercise. What job is the proper noun *Maryland* doing?

   ____

4. Find another noun in the final sentence of the exercise that is performing the same job. Write that noun and the word it is modifying.

   ____

5. Study the exercise until you are prepared for dictation.

Lesson 69

(from Exercise 69, A World of Comfort)

1. Read Exercise 69 in *Spelling Wisdom, Book 2.*
2. Identify what part of speech each italicized word is in the following sentence from the exercise. Write PRO above a pronoun, N above a common noun, PN above a proper noun, AV above an action verb, LV above a linking verb, HV above a helping verb, ADJ above an adjective, and ART above an article.

The little girl *had* already *stretched* out *her* feet to warm *them* too; but the *small flame* went

out, the *stove vanished*; she *had* only the remains of *the burnt-out match* in her hand.

3. Study the exercise until you are prepared for dictation. You will find a lot of different punctuation marks sprinkled throughout.

Lesson 70

(from Exercise 70, An Inspiration)

1. Read Exercise 70 in *Spelling Wisdom, Book 2.*
2. Identify what part of speech each italicized word is in the following sentence from the exercise. Write PRO above a pronoun, N above a common noun, PN above a proper noun, AV above an action verb, LV above a linking verb, HV above a helping verb, ADJ above an adjective, and ART above an article.

So *he returned* his *straitened* means to *his pocket* and *gave* up *the idea* of trying to buy the boys.

3. What does *straitened* mean?

____

4. Study the exercise until you are prepared for dictation.

Lesson 71

(from Exercise 71, Jumper the Hare)

1. Read Exercise 71 in *Spelling Wisdom, Book 2.*
2. Tell what a pronoun is.

____

____

3. Mark all the pronouns in these sentences from the exercise. Write PRO above each pronoun.

In summer he wears a coat of brown, but in winter he wears a coat of white, the white of the pure driven snow. So you see, he is a turncoat, but in his case it doesn't mean anything bad at all.

4. When referring to personal pronouns—like *I, you,* or *he*—the phrases *first person, second person,* and *third person* are often used. Imagine that you are standing in line, waiting for a roller coaster ride. You are the very first person in line; next to you is your friend; after him are all the other people. If you refer to yourself, you would use the pronoun *I*; as, *I can't wait!* If you address your friend next to you, the second person in line, you would use the pronoun *you*; as, *Are you ready?* And if you refer to the third person, you would use *he* or *she* (or *they* for all the rest of the people); as, *He looks scared* or *They are looking for a camera.*

   List the personal pronouns you found in the sentences from the exercise above and tell whether each is first person, second person, or third person.

____

____

____

____

5. Study the exercise until you are prepared for dictation.

Lesson 72

(from Exercise 72, With a Map)

1. Read Exercise 72 in *Spelling Wisdom, Book 2.*
2. Which pronoun is used most in the exercise?

   ____

3. The possessive form of that pronoun is also used. Write the possessive form.

   ____________________ ____________________________

4. Is that personal pronoun first person, second person, or third person?

   ____

5. Study the exercise until you are prepared for dictation. Be sure to hyphenate *such-and-such.*

Lesson 73

(from Exercise 73, The Land of Story-books)

1. Read Exercise 73 in *Spelling Wisdom, Book 2.*
2. You will find first person and third person pronouns in the exercise. Remember, if you were talking, words that refer to yourself are considered first person pronouns. List all the first person pronouns you find in the exercise.

   ____

3. Look back at Lessons 71 and 72 to review which pronouns are second person and third person. List all the third person pronouns you find in the poem.

   ____

4. Study the exercise until you are prepared for dictation. Notice the two proper nouns that should be capitalized, one of which is also hyphenated.

Lesson 74

(from Exercise 74, The Monster Trout)

1. Read Exercise 74 in *Spelling Wisdom, Book 2.*
2. Mark all the pronouns in this shortened sentence from the exercise. Write PRO above each pronoun.

One day, when a huge trout rolled half his length out of water behind my fly, small fry lost all their interest and I promised myself the joy of feeling my rod bend and tingle beneath the rush of that big trout if it took all summer.

3. Now list each personal pronoun below, according to whether it is first person, second person, or third person.
   - First person ______________________
   - Second person ______________________
   - Third person ______________________
4. Study the exercise until you are prepared for dictation.

Lesson 75

(from Exercise 75, The Crow and the Pitcher)

1. Read Exercise 75 in *Spelling Wisdom, Book 2.*
2. Identify what part of speech each italicized word is in the following sentence from the exercise. Write PRO above a pronoun, N above a common noun, PN above a proper noun, AV above an action verb, LV above a linking verb, HV above a helping verb, ADJ above an adjective, and ART above an article.

   At last, at last, *he saw* the water mount up near *him*; and after casting in *a* few *more* pebbles,

   he was able to quench his *thirst* and save *his* life.
3. Look at the personal pronouns you marked in that sentence. Are they first person, second person, or third person?

   ____
4. Study the exercise until you are prepared for dictation.

Lesson 76

(from Exercise 76, From the Declaration of Independence)

1. Read Exercise 76 in *Spelling Wisdom, Book 2.*
2. Identify what part of speech each italicized word is in the following sentence from the exercise. Write PRO above a pronoun, N above a common noun, PN above a proper noun, AV above an action verb, LV above a linking verb, HV above a helping verb, ADJ above an adjective, and ART above an article.

_We_ hold these truths to be _self-evident_: that all men are created _equal_, that _they are endowed_ by _their Creator_ with certain _unalienable_ rights, that among these _are_ life, liberty and _the_ pursuit of _happiness_.

3. Think of a synonym for each adjective you found in the sentence.

_______________ _______________

_______________ _______________

____

4. List the personal pronouns you marked and tell whether each is first person, second person, or third person. (Hint: Think about whether the pronoun is including the person who is speaking; if so, it is first person.)

____

____

____

5. Study the exercise until you are prepared for dictation. It is a good passage to memorize.

Lesson 77

(from Exercise 77, Rembrandt's Speed)

1. Read Exercise 77 in *Spelling Wisdom, Book 2.*
2. What word in the first sentence tells *how* Rembrandt worked?

   ____

3. Read that phrase "how rapidly Rembrandt worked," substituting for *rapidly* each of the words below:

   - meticulously
   - slowly
   - carelessly

   You will readily see that by the use of those words you change or modify the meaning of the word *worked*. What part of speech is *worked*?

   ____

   Words of this kind that modify the meaning of verbs are called adverbs.

4. Find the adverb in the last sentence of the exercise.

   ____

5. Study the exercise until you are prepared for dictation. Be sure to capitalize the names of all three people mentioned.

Lesson 78

(from Exercise 78, The Flower)

1. Read Exercise 78 in *Spelling Wisdom, Book 2.*
2. Tell what an adverb is.

___

3. In Lesson 77 you learned that an adverb can answer the question *How?* In Exercise 78 you will find it answering the question *Where?* In the shortened sentences from the exercise below, mark each italicized verb and adverb. Write AV above an action verb, LV above a linking verb, HV above a helping verb, and ADV above an adverb.

    The boy *ran around.*

    He *edged nearer* and *nearer* toward the pansy.

    He *hopped away* with the treasure.

4. Study the exercise until you are prepared for dictation. Note how the dashes set off an additional explanation.

Lesson 79

(from Exercise 79, The Dandelions)

1. Read Exercise 79 in *Spelling Wisdom, Book 2.*

2. Identify what part of speech each italicized word is in the following stanza from the poem. Write PRO above a pronoun, N above a common noun, PN above a proper noun, AV above an action verb, LV above a linking verb, HV above a helping verb, ADJ above an adjective, ART above an article, and ADV above an adverb.

    _We_ careless folk _the deed forgot;_

    Till one day, _idly_ walking,

    We _marked_ upon the _self-same spot_

    A crowd of veterans talking.

3. Study the exercise until you are prepared for dictation. The title of the poem holds the key to understanding it.

Lesson 80

(from Exercise 80, Ducks' Ditty)

1. Read Exercise 80 in *Spelling Wisdom, Book 2.*
2. What two questions can adverbs answer? (See Lessons 77 and 78.)

____

3. Adverbs can also answer *When?* Mark the italicized adverbs and verbs in these shortened sentences from the exercise. Write AV above an action verb, LV above a linking verb, HV above a helping verb, and ADV above an adverb.

He *had just composed* it himself.

When the ducks *stood* on their heads *suddenly*, as ducks will, he *would dive down* and *tickle* their necks.

Writing Point: *Notice how the adverbs in those sentences affect the mental picture you form as you read them. Try reading the sentences without the adverbs, then again with the adverbs. Good adverbs can help furnish more details for the imagination to picture.*

4. Study the exercise until you are prepared for dictation. Be sure to put the quotation marks around the song's title. Notice also that *Ducks'* is a plural possessive; put the apostrophe in the correct place when you write that word.

Lesson 81

(from Exercise 81, Grocer and Draper)

1. Read Exercise 81 in *Spelling Wisdom, Book 2.*
2. Why is *forty-eight* hyphenated?

____

3. What part of speech is *one-pound*?

____

4. Can you find another hyphenated adjective in the exercise?

____

5. See if you can solve the mathematic puzzle.

____

____

____

____

6. Study the exercise until you are prepared for dictation.

Lesson 82

(from Exercise 82, Stick To Your Purpose)

1. Read Exercise 82 in *Spelling Wisdom, Book 2.*
2. What three questions can adverbs answer? (See Lessons 77, 78, and 80.)

   ____

3. Adverbs can also answer *To what extent?* You will find three such adverbs in the first two sentences:

   ______________________ badly

   ______________________ soon

   ______________________ happy

   (You will find a short list of unusual adverbs on page 149.)

4. Did you notice what part of speech each of those adverbs modifies?

   ____

   ____

5. Summarize your findings by completing this sentence:

   An adverb can modify a verb, an ______________, or another ______________.

6. Study the exercise until you are prepared for dictation. Keep the letter format as you write.

Lesson 83

(from Exercise 83, The Cares of Housekeeping)

1. Read Exercise 83 in *Spelling Wisdom, Book 2.*
2. Mark the italicized adverbs and verbs in these shortened sentences from the exercise. Write AV above an action verb, LV above a linking verb, HV above a helping verb, and ADV above an adverb.

   After so much open air and excitement, the Toad *slept very soundly.*

   So the Mole and Rat *turned* to, *quietly* and *manfully.*

3. Is Exercise 83 written in present tense, past tense, or future tense?

   ___

4. Would you say it is written in first person, second person, or third person?

   ___

5. Study the exercise until you are prepared for dictation.

Lesson 84

(from Exercise 84, A Child's Mind)

1. Read Exercise 84 in *Spelling Wisdom, Book 2.*
2. Identify what part of speech each italicized word is in the following shortened sentence from the exercise. Write PRO above a pronoun, N above a common noun, PN above a proper noun, AV above an action verb, LV above a linking verb, HV above a helping verb, ADJ above an adjective, ART above an article, and ADV above an adverb.

She realized that _a child's mind is_ like a shallow brook which _ripples_ and _dances merrily_ over

the stony course of _its_ education and _reflects here_ a flower, _there_ a bush, _yonder_ a fleecy cloud.

3. Study the exercise until you are prepared for dictation.

Lesson 85

(from Exercise 85, Stones, Pebbles, and Sand)

1. Read Exercise 85 in *Spelling Wisdom, Book 2.*
2. Explain how to use commas in a series. Use the final sentence of the exercise as an example.

   ____

   ____

   ____

3. Mark the italicized adverbs and verbs in this shortened sentence from that sentence. Write AV above an action verb, LV above a linking verb, HV above a helping verb, and ADV above an adverb.

   This *is* what the streams *are doing everywhere.*

4. Study the exercise until you are prepared for dictation.

Lesson 86

(from Exercise 86, A Fable)

1. Read Exercise 86 in *Spelling Wisdom, Book 2.*
2. What does *former* mean?

   ____

3. What does *latter* mean?

   ____

4. Rewrite the third line of the fable, substituting the correct nouns from the fable for *former* and *latter.*

   ____

   ____

5. Write a moral for the fable.

   ____

   ____

6. Study the exercise until you are prepared for dictation. Pay attention to where the quoted material starts and ends.

Lesson 87

(from Exercise 87, Letter to Chopin)

1. Read Exercise 87 in *Spelling Wisdom, Book 2.*
2. In the first two sentences of the exercise
    - Find three first person pronouns ______________________
    - Find a second person pronoun ______________________
    - Find two third person pronouns ______________________
3. Is it a personal letter or a business letter? How can you tell?

    ____

4. Study the exercise until you are prepared for dictation. Chopin and Liszt were great friends. The Maison Troupenas (or House of Troupenas) was a music publishing house in Paris.

Lesson 88

(from Exercise 88, The Smileys)

1. Read Exercise 88 in *Spelling Wisdom, Book 2.*
2. Identify each mark of punctuation in this sentence from the exercise and explain why it is used.

   "Ah! Uncle," she exclaimed, "you have actually arrived on my twenty-first birthday!"

   - "Ah! ______________________________
     ____
   - Uncle," ______________________________
     ____
   - exclaimed, ______________________________
   - "you ______________________________
   - twenty-first ______________________________
   - birthday!" ______________________________
     ____

3. The first word of that sentence introduces a new part of speech: an interjection. An interjection is an independent word used in the sentence only for the purpose of expressing strong feeling. You won't see interjections often, but you will be able to recognize them easily. (You will find a short list of some interjections on page 149.) See if you can find an interjection in each of these previous exercises.

   - Exercise 38 ______________________________
   - Exercise 56 ______________________________
   - Exercise 69 ______________________________

4. Can you solve the mathematical riddle?

   ____

5. Study the exercise until you are prepared for dictation.

Lesson 89

(from Exercise 89, Eli Whitney)

1. Read Exercise 89 in *Spelling Wisdom, Book 2.*

2. Identify what part of speech each italicized word is in the following sentence from the exercise. Write PRO above a pronoun, N above a common noun, PN above a proper noun, AV above an action verb, LV above a linking verb, HV above a helping verb, ADJ above an adjective, ART above an article, and ADV above an adverb.

   It *was called* the cotton gin, and *it* did the work *so quickly* that almost overnight *the cotton industry* of the *South* was changed.

3. Study the exercise until you are prepared for dictation. Note that in that passage, *the South* is considered a proper noun and is capitalized, even though common compass directions like *north, south, east, west* are not.

Lesson 90

(from Exercise 90, Salmon)

1. Read Exercise 90 in *Spelling Wisdom, Book 2.*
2. Is Exercise 90 written in present tense, past tense, or future tense?

   ____

3. Would you say it is written in first person, second person, or third person?

   ____

Writing Point: *The tense and person you select to write in can greatly affect the tone of the composition. Think about how the exercise would sound if written in first person, as if the writer were a salmon and were telling his own story ("I spend my early days in fresh water . . . "). What if it were written in first person, future tense ("I will spend my early days in fresh water . . . ")? Ponder all your options when selecting tense and person in your writing.*

4. Find the compound adjective in the second paragraph.

   ____

5. Study the exercise until you are prepared for dictation.

Lesson 91

(from Exercise 91, The Piece of Wood)

1. Read Exercise 91 in *Spelling Wisdom, Book 2.*
2. Identify what part of speech each italicized word is in the following sentence from the exercise. Write PRO above a pronoun, N above a common noun, PN above a proper noun, AV above an action verb, LV above a linking verb, HV above a helping verb, ADJ above an adjective, ART above an article, and ADV above an adverb.

I *do not know* how this *really* happened, yet *the fact* remains that one *fine* day this piece of

wood found *itself* in the shop of *an* old carpenter.

3. The dash in the first line of the passage is indicating an abrupt interruption. Why is the second dash there? What is it indicating?

____

____

4. Study the exercise until you are prepared for dictation. *Mastro* is Italian for *boss* or *master*.

Lesson 92

(from Exercise 92, Psalm 46)

1. Read Exercise 92 in *Spelling Wisdom, Book 2.*
2. For each personal pronoun from the exercise, tell whether it is first person, second person, or third person.

    - Our ____________________
    - We ____________________
    - Her ____________________
    - She ____________________
    - He ____________________
    - His ____________________
    - Us ____________________
    - I ____________________

3. Study the exercise until you are prepared for dictation. Take careful note of all the words that are capitalized because they refer to deity. The exact meaning of *Selah* is not known, but we think it was a musical directive that provided opportunity for the worshipers to pause and think about the words.

Lesson 93

(from Exercise 93, Armistice Day)

1. Read Exercise 93 in *Spelling Wisdom, Book 2.*
2. Sometimes you will find a phrase, a group of words, that is doing the work of an adverb or an adjective. Look closely at the two italicized phrases in the sentence from the exercise.

   The armistice had been signed *at five o'clock* that morning, and the war *with Germany* was over.

   Which phrase is doing the work of an adverb?

   ____

3. What verb is it modifying?

   ____

4. Which phrase is doing the work of an adjective?

   ____

5. What noun is it modifying?

   ____

6. Study the exercise until you are prepared for dictation. Be sure to include the apostrophes in the two phrases that indicate time of day.

Lesson 94

(from Exercise 94, The Businessman)

1. Read Exercise 94 in *Spelling Wisdom, Book 2.*
2. Look closely at the two italicized phrases in the sentence from the exercise.

   At a tiny little place* in New York City, his workers make model airplanes *for the government.

   What word does the first phrase modify?

   ____

3. What part of speech is that word?

   ____

4. So is the phrase doing the work of an adverb or an adjective?

   ____

5. What word does the second phrase modify?

   ____

6. What part of speech is that word?

   ____

7. Is the second phrase doing the work of an adverb or an adjective?

   ____

8. Study the exercise until you are prepared for dictation. Be sure to capitalize all of the proper nouns.

Lesson 95

(from Exercise 95, The Kingfisher's Den)

1. Read Exercise 95 in *Spelling Wisdom, Book 2.*
2. For each italicized phrase in the sentence from the exercise tell whether it is doing the work of an adjective or an adverb and what word it is modifying.

   All who have ever watched the bird have, no doubt, noticed his wonderful ability to stop short *in swift flight* and hold himself poised in midair *for an indefinite time*, while watching the movements *of a minnow* beneath.

   - In swift flight ______________________________
   - For an indefinite time ______________________________
   - Of a minnow ______________________________

3. Study the exercise until you are prepared for dictation.

Lesson 96

(from Exercise 96, A Little Old Trunk)

1. Read Exercise 96 in *Spelling Wisdom, Book 2.*
2. What is Mary's last name?

 ____

3. How can you tell whether the *s* is part of the name?

 ____

4. Why is there no *s* after the apostrophe that denotes possession?

 ____

5. Find three more possessive proper nouns in the last paragraph of the exercise. Rewrite each name and what belonged to that person as a phrase: the [possession] belonging to [proper noun].

 - ____
 - ____
 - ____

Writing Point: *This is a great exercise to do when writing possessive nouns to make sure you are communicating clearly.*

6. Study the exercise until you are prepared for dictation. Be sure to put the apostrophes in their correct places.

Lesson 97

(from Exercise 97, Meters)

1. Read Exercise 97 in *Spelling Wisdom, Book 2.*
2. Find the interjection in the final sentence of the exercise.

   ____

3. Why are there three quotation marks at the beginning of the fourth line?

   ____

   ____

4. Demonstrate how to properly punctuate a sentence when the dialogue tag comes after the quoted material, before the quoted material, between two sentences, and splits a sentence. The first one is done for you as an example.

   "Quoted material," dialogue tag.

   Dialogue tag Quoted material

   Quoted sentence dialogue tag Quoted sentence

   Quoted sentence begins dialogue tag rest of quoted sentence

   Writing Point: *If you enjoy writing fiction, you especially need to learn how to punctuate dialogue correctly.*

5. Study the exercise until you are prepared for dictation.

Lesson 98

(from Exercise 98, Concord Hymn)

1. Read Exercise 98 in *Spelling Wisdom, Book 2.*
2. For each italicized phrase in the lines from the poem tell whether it is doing the work of an adjective or an adverb and what word it is modifying. Think about what question each phrase answers.

   By the rude bridge **that arched the flood,**

   Their flag to April's breeze unfurled,

   Here once the embattled farmers stood,

   And fired the shot heard ***round the world.***

   - By the rude bridge ____________________
   - Round the world ____________________

   On this green bank, by this soft stream,

   We set today a votive stone;

   - On this green bank ____________________
   - By this soft stream ____________________

3. Study the exercise until you are prepared for dictation. Emerson wrote that poem in 1837 to be sung at a ceremony that was held when the Concord Monument in Massachusetts was completed. The monument reminds people of the Minutemen's stand against British forces near the towns of Lexington and Concord and how important that battle was in the American Revolution.

Lesson 99

(from Exercise 99, The Butterfly and the Crocodile)

1. Read Exercise 99 in *Spelling Wisdom, Book 2.*
2. In each italicized phrase from the sentence in the exercise underline its principal word and tell what part of speech that word is. The first phrase is done for you.

   It flew with careless ease *over the back of a crocodile* stretched out *on a dry bank* and taking a nap *in the sun.*

   - Over the back: noun
   - Of a crocodile ______________________________
   - On a dry bank ______________________________
   - In the sun ______________________________

   The little words that introduce the phrases (namely, *over, of, on, in*) are called prepositions. Prepositions not only introduce phrases, but they show the relation between the principal word of the phrase and some other word in the sentence. You will find a short list of commonly used prepositions on page 149.
3. Study the exercise until you are prepared for dictation.

Lesson 100

(from Exercise 100, Minstrels)

1. Read Exercise 100 in *Spelling Wisdom, Book 2.*
2. What is a preposition? (See Lesson 99.)

   ____

   ____

   ____

3. Identify the three prepositions in the italicized phrases in the following sentence from the exercise. Write PP above each preposition that begins the phrase. Also identify the parts of speech for the other words in the phrases: write ART above an article, ADJ above an adjective, N above a noun, PRO above a pronoun.

   A minstrel who found favor *with a king* might remain *for some time at court.*

4. Look at your markings and complete this sentence:

   In a prepositional phrase, the principal word will usually be a ____________________.

5. Study the exercise until you are prepared for dictation.

Lesson 101

(from Exercise 101, Orioles)

1. Read Exercise 101 in *Spelling Wisdom, Book 2.*
2. Identify the parts of speech of the italicized words in the sentence from the exercise. Write PP above each preposition that begins the phrase, ART above an article, ADJ above an adjective, N above a noun, PRO above a pronoun.

   The number *of grubs, worms, flies, caterpillars,* and even cocoons that go to satisfy the hunger *of a family* of orioles *in a day* might indicate, if it could be computed, the great value these birds are *about our homes,* aside from the good cheer they bring.

3. Study the exercise until you are prepared for dictation.

Lesson 102

(from Exercise 102, Crossword Puzzle)

1. Read Exercise 102 in *Spelling Wisdom, Book 2.*
2. Why are the exclamation point and question mark inside the quotation marks in these sentences from the exercise?

   "Suppose I get stuck?" laughed Judy. "There are such hard words here!"

   ____

   ____

3. Why are the exclamation point and question mark outside the quotation marks in these sentences from the exercise?

   Was it "mailbox"? Oh, no. It is "envelope"!

   ____

   ____

4. Contrast that guideline with the placement of the periods at the end of these sentences.

   "Next after eighth" was, of course, "ninth."

   At last she wrote "ans.," "division," and "dozen."

   Can you come up with a guideline for the placement of periods with quotation marks?

   ____

   ____

5. Study the exercise until you are prepared for dictation. Be especially mindful of the punctuation.

Lesson 103

(from Exercise 103, A New Colt)

1. Read Exercise 103 in *Spelling Wisdom, Book 2.*
2. Identify what part of speech each italicized word is in the following sentence from the exercise. Write PRO above a pronoun, N above a common noun, PN above a proper noun, AV above an action verb, LV above a linking verb, HV above a helping verb, ADJ above an adjective, ART above an article, ADV above an adverb, PP above a preposition that begins a phrase.

After a week or two, when the *weather* was warmer, *the youngest colt* and *his* mother *were*

allowed outside in a small field behind the stable.

Writing Point: *To communicate clearly, try to keep prepositional phrases near the words they modify in the sentence. You'll be able to see for yourself how things can get confusing if you take the two prepositional phrases you marked ("in a small field" and "behind the stable") and shift one or both to different places in the sentence.*

3. Study the exercise until you are prepared for dictation.

Lesson 104

(from Exercise 104, Lunch in Pairs)

1. Read Exercise 104 in *Spelling Wisdom, Book 2.*
2. Identify what part of speech each italicized word is in the following sentence from the exercise. Write PRO above a pronoun, N above a common noun, PN above a proper noun, AV above an action verb, LV above a linking verb, HV above a helping verb, ADJ above an adjective, ART above an article, ADV above an adverb, PP above a preposition that begins a phrase.

   Twelve men **connected with a large firm** ***in the city of London sit down*** **to luncheon together**

   every day ***in the same room.***

3. Try the mathematics challenge.
4. Study the exercise until you are prepared for dictation.

Lesson 105

(from Exercise 105, Be Peace-Possessed)

1. Read Exercise 105 in *Spelling Wisdom, Book 2.*
2. Is Exercise 105 written in present tense, past tense, or future tense?

   ____

3. Would you say it is written in first person, second person, or third person?

   ____

4. Can you find three prepositional phrases back to back in the following sentence? Underline them.

   Bubble over with suppressed excitement and the deer yonder, stepping daintily down the bank to your canoe in the water grasses, will stamp and snort and bound away without ever knowing what startled him.

5. What is a kickshaw? Be sure to select the definition that best fits the context.

   ____

   ____

6. Study the exercise until you are prepared for dictation.

Lesson 106

(from Exercise 106, The Brook)

1. Read Exercise 106 in *Spelling Wisdom, Book 2.*

2. Now it is time to learn the final part of speech. You are quite familiar with the noun, the pronoun, the adjective, the article, the verb, the adverb, the preposition, and the interjection. A conjunction is a connecting word. It can connect single words or groups of words. You will find a short list of frequently used conjunctions on page 149. Look closely at the following lines of the poem to find a popular conjunction. It is used several times.

   Cool and clear and free,

   Swift, and strong, and happy,

   Flecked with shade and sun.

   Conjunction ______________________

3. Study the exercise until you are prepared for dictation.

Lesson 107

(from Exercise 107, More About Brooks)

1. Read Exercise 107 in *Spelling Wisdom, Book 2.*
2. Identify what part of speech each word is in the following sentence from the exercise. Write PRO above a pronoun, N above a common noun, PN above a proper noun, AV above an action verb, LV above a linking verb, HV above a helping verb, ADJ above an adjective, ART above an article, ADV above an adverb, PP above a preposition that begins a phrase, and CON above a conjunction.

The water is clear, and the soil has settled to the bottom.

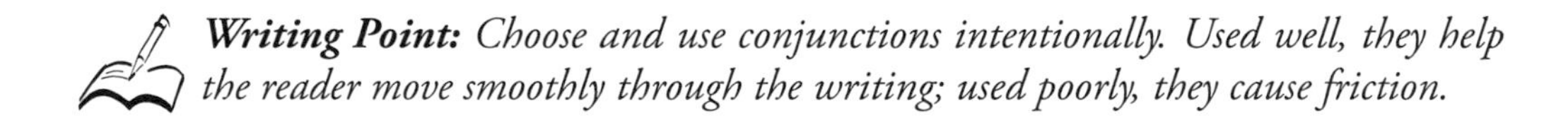

Writing Point: *Choose and use conjunctions intentionally. Used well, they help the reader move smoothly through the writing; used poorly, they cause friction.*

3. Study the exercise until you are prepared for dictation.

Lesson 108

(from Exercise 108, A Colonial Kitchen)

1. Read Exercise 108 in *Spelling Wisdom, Book 2.*
2. Define each word listed below, then without looking at the exercise, determine which homonym from each set belongs in the given statements.

   - need ________________
   - knead ________________
   - to ________________
   - too ________________
   - two ________________

   Every kind of pan and every spoon used to stir food was made with a very long handle so that the cook ________ not stoop nor get ________ close ________ the fire.

   - would ________________
   - wood ________________
   - their ________________
   - there ________________
   - they're ________________
   - meats ________________
   - meets ________________

   They ________ either boil or roast ________ ________ and would mix all the vegetables together for boiling.

3. Study the exercise until you are prepared for dictation.

Lesson 109

(from Exercise 109, Colonial Dishes)

1. Read Exercise 109 in *Spelling Wisdom, Book 2.*
2. Identify what part of speech each word is in the following sentence from the exercise. Write PRO above a pronoun, N above a common noun, PN above a proper noun, AV above an action verb, LV above a linking verb, HV above a helping verb, ADJ above an adjective, ART above an article, ADV above an adverb, PP above a preposition that begins a phrase, and CON above a conjunction.

Husband and wife used one trencher, and two children ate from one.

3. Study the exercise until you are prepared for dictation. You will find several series with the items separated by commas.

Lesson 110

(from Exercise 110, The Fox and the Cat)

1. Read Exercise 110 in *Spelling Wisdom, Book 2.*

2. Look closely at the title of the exercise. Notice which words are capitalized and which are not. Also notice which parts of speech the non-capitalized words are. Based on what you see, come up with a potential guideline for capitalizing titles.

   ____

   ____

3. Check the titles of these other exercises to see if your guideline holds true; adjust it as needed: 1, 5, 12, 16, 22, 25, 27, 36, 44, 52, 57.

   ____

   ____

4. Study the exercise until you are prepared for dictation. Pay special attention to the dialogue punctuation and capitalization.

Lesson 111

(from Exercise 111, The Chimney Swift)

1. Read Exercise 111 in *Spelling Wisdom, Book 2.*
2. Identify what part of speech each italicized word is in the following sentence from the exercise. Write PRO above a pronoun, N above a common noun, PN above a proper noun, AV above an action verb, LV above a linking verb, HV above a helping verb, ADJ above an adjective, ART above an article, ADV above an adverb, PP above a preposition that begins a phrase, and CON above a conjunction.

With *this* he *glues* the *little* twigs *together and* fastens *them to the bricks.*

3. Find the compound adjective in the first sentence.

____

4. Study the exercise until you are prepared for dictation.

Lesson 112

(from Exercise 112, Doing Chores)

1. Read Exercise 112 in *Spelling Wisdom, Book 2.*
2. Identify what part of speech each italicized word is in the following sentence from the exercise. Write PRO above a pronoun, N above a common noun, PN above a proper noun, AV above an action verb, LV above a linking verb, HV above a helping verb, ADJ above an adjective, ART above an article, ADV above an adverb, PP above a preposition that begins a phrase, and CON above a conjunction.

   In the living room* she had to sweep the floor *and rub* wax *over it* and dust the furniture *with a clean rag.

3. What is a harrow?

   ____

   ____

4. Study the exercise until you are prepared for dictation.

Lesson 113

(from Exercise 113, Arithmetic Spelling)

1. Read Exercise 113 in *Spelling Wisdom, Book 2.*
2. Why are there both a period and a comma inside the quotation marks in the third sentence?

   ____

   ____

3. Why do the following words have hyphens?
   - two-word ____
   - twenty-one ____
   - twenty-nine ____
4. Why is *borrow one* in quotation marks?

   ____

   ____

5. Study the exercise until you are prepared for dictation.

Lesson 114

(from Exercise 114, The Gardener)

1. Read Exercise 114 in *Spelling Wisdom, Book 2.*
2. Identify what part of speech each italicized word is in the following stanza from the poem. Write PRO above a pronoun, N above a common noun, PN above a proper noun, AV above an action verb, LV above a linking verb, HV above a helping verb, ADJ above an adjective, ART above an article, ADV above an adverb, PP above a preposition that begins a phrase, CON above a conjunction, and INT above an interjection.

Silly gardener! summer *goes,*

And winter comes *with pinching toes,*

When in *the* garden *bare* and *brown*

You must lay your barrow *down.*

3. Study the exercise until you are prepared for dictation. Make sure you spell the fruit, *currant,* found in the garden and not the time designation, *current.*

Lesson 115

(from Exercise 115, Sailing Ships)

1. Read Exercise 115 in *Spelling Wisdom, Book 2.*

2. You already know that a sentence can be divided into two main parts: the subject (that of which we speak) and the predicate (what we say about it). Divide this sentence from the exercise into its two main parts by drawing a line between the subject and the predicate.

   Commerce with England and the West Indies went forward by leaps and bounds.

3. When we keep all the words in the subject and predicate, they are called the complete subject and complete predicate. But now that you know the parts of speech, you can peel off the extra words to find the one or two crucial words that boil the sentence down to just its essentials: its simple subject and predicate.

   Look at the complete subject part of the sentence you marked above. Remove the prepositional phrase; the noun that remains alone is the simple subject.

   ____

   Look at the complete predicate part of the sentence. Remove the adverb and the prepositional phrase; the verb that remains alone is the simple predicate.

   ____

4. Study the exercise until you are prepared for dictation.

Lesson 116

(from Exercise 116, Over the Bridge)

1. Read Exercise 116 in *Spelling Wisdom, Book 2.*

2. Find the simple subject and predicate of this shortened sentence from the exercise by identifying the complete subject and predicate, then removing all words and phrases that modify until you have the simple subject noun and the simple predicate verb remaining alone. Feel free to identify and label the parts of speech used in the sentence if it will help you.

   A prolonged screech issued from the locomotive.

   - Simple subject ______________________________

   - Simple predicate ______________________________

3. Study the exercise until you are prepared for dictation. If you have not yet read *Around the World in Eighty Days*, you are missing a treat!

Lesson 117

(from Exercise 117, Fresh Deer Tracks)

1. Read Exercise 117 in *Spelling Wisdom, Book 2.*
2. Find the simple subject and predicate of this sentence from the exercise. Feel free to identify and label the parts of speech used in the sentence if it will help you.

   My heart jumped at sight of one great hoof mark.

   - Simple subject ______________________________
   - Simple predicate ______________________________

3. What does *browse* mean in the context of that passage?

   ____

   ____

4. Study the exercise until you are prepared for dictation.

Lesson 118

(from Exercise 118, American Independence)

1. Read Exercise 118 in *Spelling Wisdom, Book 2.*
2. Notice the three dates in the exercise. What capitalization and punctuation guidelines apply when writing dates into sentences?
3. Alphabetize the sixteen proper nouns found in the exercise. Keep multi-word proper nouns together and treat them as one entry; e.g., British Empire. Be sure to write and arrange the two persons' names as *Last, First* in your list.
4. Study the exercise until you are prepared for dictation.

Lesson 119

(from Exercise 119, Writing an Essay)

1. Read Exercise 119 in *Spelling Wisdom, Book 2.*
2. In the sentence below, the subject is not expressed at all. Remove all the prepositional phrases and what do you have left?

   ____

   Go to a library to find books and articles from current magazines on your topic.

3. What is the author's intent? Whom is he addressing with that sentence?

   ____

   Though only the predicate of the sentence is expressed, *you* is the subject just as truly as though it were printed in front of the predicate. The sentence means *You go to a library.* When we identify the simple subject of a sentence of that kind we say the subject is *you (understood).* Look at Exercises 1, 6, and 107 to see other sentences in which the subject is *you (understood).*

4. Find at least four more sentences in Exercise 119 that have a subject of *you (understood).*

   ____

   ____

   ____

   ____

   ____

   ____

   ____

5. Study the exercise until you are prepared for dictation.

Lesson 120

(from Exercise 120, Bartering Animals)

1. Read Exercise 120 in *Spelling Wisdom, Book 2.*
2. Find the simple subject and predicate of this sentence from the exercise. Feel free to identify and label the parts of speech used in the sentence if it will help you.

   Three countrymen met at a cattle market.

   - Simple subject ______________________________
   - Simple predicate ______________________________

3. See if you can solve the mathematical riddle.

   ____

   ____

   ____

4. Study the exercise until you are prepared for dictation. Note the semicolon used in the final dialogue passage.

Lesson 121

(from Exercise 121, The Death of Lincoln)

1. Read Exercise 121 in *Spelling Wisdom, Book 2.*

2. Thus far when identifying the simple subject and predicate, the subject has stood close to the beginning of the sentence. Not so with the following two statements from the poem. Find the simple subject and predicate of each. Don't be fooled by where the words stand. Look closely and determine what each sentence speaks of and what is said about it, eliminate extra modifiers, and pare the statements down to their essentials. Feel free to identify and label the parts of speech if it will help you.

In sorrow by thy bier we stand.

- Simple subject ______________________________

- Simple predicate ______________________________

Pure was thy life.

- Simple subject ______________________________

- Simple predicate ______________________________

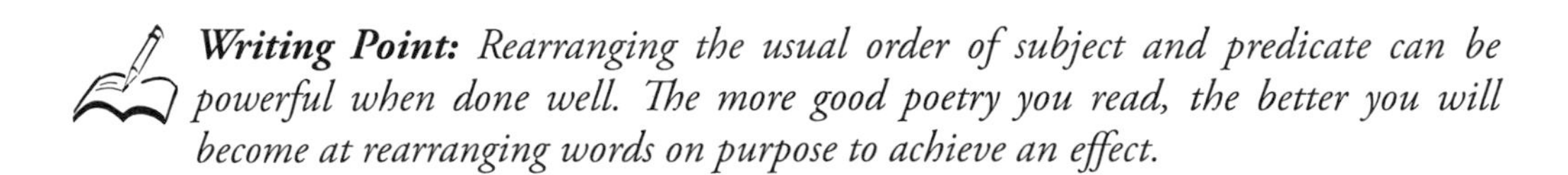

Writing Point: *Rearranging the usual order of subject and predicate can be powerful when done well. The more good poetry you read, the better you will become at rearranging words on purpose to achieve an effect.*

3. Study the exercise until you are prepared for dictation.

Lesson 122

(from Exercise 122, English Sparrows)

1. Read Exercise 122 in *Spelling Wisdom, Book 2.*
2. Identify what part of speech each italicized word is in the following stanza from the poem. Write PRO above a pronoun, N above a common noun, PN above a proper noun, AV above an action verb, LV above a linking verb, HV above a helping verb, ADJ above an adjective, ART above an article, ADV above an adverb, PP above a preposition that begins a phrase, CON above a conjunction, and INT above an interjection.

The English sparrow, or finch, as he is _more properly_ called, _may be a troublesome_ visitor, _but_

we invited him to come, _and_ he is _not_ to blame for some _of his disagreeable ways._

3. Study the exercise until you are prepared for dictation. The English sparrow is also called a house sparrow.

Lesson 123

(from Exercise 123, The Constitution)

1. Read Exercise 123 in *Spelling Wisdom, Book 2.*

2. Notice the punctuation used in this list in sentence form.

   The first three articles state: first, that the legislative power should be in the hands of Congress; second, that the executive power should be in the hands of the President of the United States; and third, that the judicial power should be in the hands of the Supreme Court.

   What does the colon indicate?

   ____

3. What job are the semicolons doing?

   ____

4. What job is the period doing?

   ____

5. What do you notice about the three commas' placement in the list?

   ____

   ____

6. Study the exercise until you are prepared for dictation. Note the consistent and similar structure of all three points' wording: *first, second, third.*

Lesson 124

(from Exercise 124, Work on the Prairie)

1. Read Exercise 124 in *Spelling Wisdom, Book 2.*
2. Define each word listed below, then without looking at the exercise, determine which homonym from each set belongs in the given sentence.

   - blue ______________________________
   - blew ______________ ______________
   - dye ______________________________
   - die ______________________________

   Her mother had woven the material, and the ____________ ____________ had come from Boston.

3. Write Mary's first and last name.

   ____________ ______________________ ________

4. How would you write her name as a possessive, showing that she had a new cap and coat?

   ____

5. Study the exercise until you are prepared for dictation.

Lesson 125

(from Exercise 125, Grandmother's Cookbook)

1. Read Exercise 125 in *Spelling Wisdom, Book 2.*
2. Identify each mark of punctuation in the following sentences from the exercise and explain why it is used.

   The first part of the cookbook contained recipes for making pickles: sweet pickles, sour pickles, watermelon pickles, and spiced fruits. Grandmother had written a note on one recipe, "Not too much celery seed next time. H.R. (Grandfather) doesn't like it."

   - pickles: ______________________________
   - sweet pickles, ______________________________
   - sour pickles, ______________________________
   - watermelon pickles, ______________________________
   - fruits. ______________________________
   - recipe, ______________________________
   - "Not ______________________________
   - time. ______________________________
   - H. R. ______________________________
   - (Grandfather) ______________________________
   - doesn't ______________________________
   - it." ______________________________

   ____

3. Study the exercise until you are prepared for dictation.

Lesson 126

(from Exercise 126, Buttons Learns to Jump)

1. Read Exercise 126 in *Spelling Wisdom, Book 2.*
2. In the exercise find
    - A hyphenated adjective ______________________
    - A series divided by commas ______________________
    - A singular possessive proper noun ______________________
    - A singular possessive common noun ______________________
    - An interjection ______________________
    - Three different conjunctions ______________________

 ***Writing Point:*** *Have you used any interjections in your written narrations lately?*

3. Study the exercise until you are prepared for dictation.

Lesson 127

(from Exercise 127, Thanksgiving Proclamation)

1. Read Exercise 127 in *Spelling Wisdom, Book 2.*
2. Notice how many sentences the exercise is comprised of.

   ____

3. One word in the exercise is often mistaken for a word that looks similar but has a different meaning. Define both words below.

   • conscience ______________________________

   ____

   • conscious ______________________________

   ____

4. Why does *conscience* fit best in the phrase "freedom to worship God according to the dictates of our own conscience"?

   ____

   ____

   ____

5. The wording will be a bit unusual because of the time period in which that proclamation was written. Pay close attention as you study the exercise and prepare it for dictation.

Lesson 128

(from Exercise 128, The Blue Jay)

1. Read Exercise 128 in *Spelling Wisdom, Book 2.*

2. Identify what part of speech each italicized word is in the following sentence from the exercise. Write PRO above a pronoun, N above a common noun, PN above a proper noun, AV above an action verb, LV above a linking verb, HV above a helping verb, ADJ above an adjective, ART above an article, ADV above an adverb, PP above a preposition that begins a phrase, CON above a conjunction, and INT above an interjection.

   No bird *of finer color or presence sojourns* with *us* the year round than *the blue jay.*

3. Study the exercise until you are prepared for dictation.

Lesson 129

(from Exercise 129, Major C)

1. Read Exercise 129 in *Spelling Wisdom, Book 2.*
2. Find an antonym in the exercise for each word below.
    - enlargement ____________________
    - dim ____________________
    - failure ____________________
    - civilian ____________________
    - tarnished ____________________
    - elderly ____________________
    - insincere ____________________
3. Study the exercise until you are prepared for dictation.

Lesson 130

(from Exercise 130, Egyptian Pyramids)

1. Read Exercise 130 in *Spelling Wisdom, Book 2.*
2. Rewrite each of these phrases as a possessive word and what it possessed. For example, *pyramids of pharaohs* would become *pharaohs' pyramids.* Be watchful to place apostrophes correctly.
    - time of ten weeks ____________________
    - tomb of it ____________________
    - mummies of kings ____________________
    - mummies of animals ____________________
    - mummies of people ____________________
3. Study the exercise until you are prepared for dictation.

Lesson 131

(from Exercise 131, Tookhees the Mouse)

1. Read Exercise 131 in *Spelling Wisdom, Book 2.*

2. Identify what part of speech each italicized word is in the following sentence from the exercise. Write PRO above a pronoun, N above a common noun, PN above a proper noun, AV above an action verb, LV above a linking verb, HV above a helping verb, ADJ above an adjective, ART above an article, ADV above an adverb, PP above a preposition that begins a phrase, CON above a conjunction, and INT above an interjection.

   But **he** ***was suspicious of the big object, or*** **perhaps he** ***smelled*** **the man too** ***and*** **was afraid,** ***for***

   after much dodging in and out ***he*** **disappeared** ***altogether.***

3. Study the exercise until you are prepared for dictation.

Lesson 132

(from Exercise 132, A Tapestry)

1. Read Exercise 132 in *Spelling Wisdom, Book 2.*

2. Find the simple subject and predicate of each of these sentences from the exercise. Feel free to identify and label the parts of speech if it will help you.

   The colors are bright.

   - Simple subject ____________________

   - Simple predicate ____________________

   Such tapestries served a double purpose.

   - Simple subject ____________________

   - Simple predicate ____________________

3. The sentence below contains a compound subject—two words of equal importance connected by a conjunction. Find the compound subject.

   The floors and walls of castles were paved with stone.

   - Compound subject ____________________

4. Study the exercise until you are prepared for dictation.

Lesson 133

(from Exercise 133, The Savanna Sparrow)

1. Read Exercise 133 in *Spelling Wisdom, Book 2.*
2. Give the definition and one example from the exercise for each part of speech listed below.

   - Common noun ______________________________

     ____

   - Proper noun ______________________________

     ____

   - Pronoun ______________________________

     ____

   - Action verb ______________________________

     ____

   - Linking verb ______________________________

     ____

   - Helping verb ______________________________

     ____

3. Study the exercise until you are prepared for dictation.

Lesson 134

(from Exercise 134, Glimpse of the Big Buck)

1. Read Exercise 134 in *Spelling Wisdom, Book 2.*
2. For each pronoun listed below, give its antecedent and tell whether it is singular or plural.
   - I ______________________________
   - they ______________________________
   - their ______________________________
   - your ______________________________
   - he ______________________________
   - one ______________________________
3. Study the exercise until you are prepared for dictation.

Lesson 135

(from Exercise 135, God Save the Queen)

1. Read Exercise 135 in *Spelling Wisdom, Book 2.*
2. Define each word listed below, then without looking at the exercise, determine which homonym from each set belongs in the given lines from the poem.

   - our ____________________
   - hour ____________________

   God save ____________ gracious Queen!

   - reign ____________________
   - rein ____________________
   - rain ____________________

   Long to ____________ over us,

   - pour ____________________
   - poor ____________________
   - pore ____________________

   On her be pleased to ____________;

   - see ____________________
   - sea ____________________

   Lord make the nations ____________,

   - one ____________________
   - won ____________________

   And form ____________ family,

3. Study the exercise until you are prepared for dictation.

Lesson 136

(from Exercise 136, The Way We Go)

1. Read Exercise 136 in *Spelling Wisdom, Book 2.*

2. Identify what part of speech each italicized word is in the following sentence from the exercise. Write PRO above a pronoun, N above a common noun, PN above a proper noun, AV above an action verb, LV above a linking verb, HV above a helping verb, ADJ above an adjective, ART above an article, ADV above an adverb, PP above a preposition that begins a phrase, CON above a conjunction, and INT above an interjection.

We *would not feel* comfortable if a big barbarian came *into our quiet home*, broke the door down, whacked *his* war-club *on the furniture, and* whooped his battle *yell.*

3. Explain why the commas are placed where they are in the sentence.

____

____

4. Study the exercise until you are prepared for dictation. Notice the author used *Wood Folk* as a proper noun and capitalized it.

Lesson 137

(from Exercise 137, Traveling East)

1. Read Exercise 137 in *Spelling Wisdom, Book 2.*
2. Give the definition and one example from the exercise for each part of speech listed below.
   - Adjective ______________________________
     ____
   - Article ______________________________
     ____
   - Adverb ______________________________
     ____
   - Conjunction ______________________________
     ____
3. Is Exercise 137 written in present tense, past tense, or future tense?
   ____
4. Would you say it is written in first person, second person, or third person?
   ____
5. Study the exercise until you are prepared for dictation.

Lesson 138

(from Exercise 138, Up We Go!)

1. Read Exercise 138 in *Spelling Wisdom, Book 2.*
2. How many prepositions can you find in the following sentence from the exercise? Write PP above each.

The Mole had been working very hard all the morning, spring-cleaning his little home—first with brooms, then with dusters, then on ladders and steps and chairs, with a brush and a pail of whitewash—till he had dust in his throat and eyes, and splashes of whitewash all over his black fur, and an aching back and weary arms.

3. Find three interjections in the exercise.

____

____

4. Study the exercise until you are prepared for dictation.

Lesson 139

(from Exercise 139, The Town Mouse and the Country Mouse)

1. Read Exercise 139 in *Spelling Wisdom, Book 2.*

2. Find the simple subject and compound predicate of this sentence from the exercise. Feel free to identify and label the parts of speech if it will help you. You found a compound subject in Lesson 132. A compound predicate is somewhat similar; it will have two verbs of equal importance connected by a conjunction.

   The two mice set off for the town and arrived at the Town Mouse's residence late at night.

   - Simple subject ____

   - Compound predicate ____

3. Study the exercise until you are prepared for dictation.

Lesson 140

(from Exercise 140, Story of the Raindrops)

1. Read Exercise 140 in *Spelling Wisdom, Book 2.*
2. Identify what part of speech each italicized word is in the following sentence from the exercise. Write PRO above a pronoun, N above a common noun, PN above a proper noun, AV above an action verb, LV above a linking verb, HV above a helping verb, ADJ above an adjective, ART above an article, ADV above an adverb, PP above a preposition that begins a phrase, CON above a conjunction, and INT above an interjection.

When we got pretty high where the _air was cool, we came_ closer together again _and_ formed

_a_ great fleecy _white_ cloud that cast _its_ shadow _over everything._

3. Study the exercise until you are prepared for dictation.

Parts of Speech Short Lists

Some Pronouns Frequently Used

I	we	you	he	she	it	they	who	which
mine	ours	yours	his	hers		theirs	whom	what
me	us		him	her		them		that

Some Verbs Often Used as Helping Verbs

am	are	is	been	was	were
have	has	had	do	does	did
shall	should	will	would		
can	could	may	might	must	

Some Unusual Adverbs

Besides those that answer How? Where? When? *and* To what extent?, *the following words can also be adverbs.*

yes	no	therefore
certainly	not	consequently
	never	

Some Prepositions Commonly Used

above	by	into	up
across	down	of	upon
at	for	on	under
before	from	over	with
behind	in	to	without

Some Conjunctions Commonly Used

and	as	because	until
but	if	since	when
or	for	unless	while

Some Interjections Commonly Used

O	ah	alas	hark
oh	ay	hurrah	lo